IMAGES
of America

OKLAHOMA CITY
RADIO

The full-time staff of WKY Radio in 1937 gathers in the foyer of the fourth floor of the Skirvin Tower Hotel, the home of WKY. In addition to all these people, an equal number who were either part time or contract employees, such as musicians, actors, actresses, and singers were also required for the various programs the station broadcast daily and weekly. (Courtesy Oklahoma Historical Society.)

ON THE COVER: Danny Williams hosted the morning show in the mid-1960s on WKY Radio. Williams was the only DJ to host number-one rated morning shows on three different radio stations in Oklahoma City. After leaving WKY, he took the morning show at KEBC, the country music FM station, then in the early 1990s, he took the morning show at KOMA to number one playing oldies. Williams also hosted two daily shows on WKY-TV, later KTVY after the station was sold. (Courtesy Oklahoma Historical Society.)

IMAGES of America
OKLAHOMA CITY RADIO

Michael Dean

*Tyler and Mary Turner -
Enjoy the book and
Boomer Sooner!
Michael*

ARCADIA
PUBLISHING

Copyright © 2019 by Michael Dean
ISBN 978-1-4671-0343-5

Published by Arcadia Publishing
Charleston, South Carolina

Printed in the United States of America

Library of Congress Control Number: 2019936667

For all general information, please contact Arcadia Publishing:
Telephone 843-853-2070
Fax 843-853-0044
E-mail sales@arcadiapublishing.com
For customer service and orders:
Toll-Free 1-888-313-2665

Visit us on the Internet at www.arcadiapublishing.com

CONTENTS

Acknowledgments		6
Introduction		7
1.	In the Beginning	11
2.	WKY and KOMA Become Big-Time Radio Stations	23
3.	One of America's Biggest Rock 'n' Roll Radio Battles	43
4.	The Day the Music Died	67
5.	Today in Oklahoma City Radio	79

Acknowledgments

I landed my first job in radio during my junior year at Broken Bow High School, working three nights a week at KBEL Radio in Idabel, Oklahoma. That was in 1964. My last full-time job in radio was at KOMA, where I was the music director and "Dean of Rock 'n' Roll." I was part of the staff that flipped the station to oldies in 1988. Within a year, we were one of the highest-rated oldies station in the country playing music on an AM radio station.

In 2003, I became the director of public relations at the Oklahoma Historical Society (OHS), where Dr. Bob Blackburn was executive director. He had grown up around television in Oklahoma City, as his mother had raised him and his sister as a single parent while working at KOCO-TV hosting a variety of programs. He had an interest in the history of Oklahoma broadcasting, but his PhD in Oklahoma history followed other courses. He knew of my interest and encouraged me to pursue the histories of various stations and companies. Eventually, he began to refer to me as "Oklahoma's Broadcast Historian." I am very grateful for his encouragement and help.

The photographs in this book are all from collections in the Archives Division of the OHS. Chad Williams, the division director, spent many hours helping me find specific photographs and scanning them for this publication.

Jack Sampson was the first general manager of KOMA when Todd Storz bought the station in 1958 and promoted Sampson from sales manager at his Kansas City station WHB. Sampson donated a number of photographs from his collection to the OHS and spent many hours with me sharing stories of his years in Oklahoma City at KOMA. He introduced me to Deane Johnson, who was the second rock and roll program director at KOMA. He also donated photographs and shared stories from his years in Oklahoma City.

WKY was owned by *Daily Oklahoman* owner E.K. Gaylord. I worked with Danny Williams, who had been a longtime employee of WKY Radio and TV. Williams donated many items and photographs to the OHS and shared his memories.

Ralph Tyler and his sons Ty and Tony are pioneers in Oklahoma City radio. Ralph developed the first FM station that was rated number one in Oklahoma City, and his sons have followed by starting two FM stations and two television stations that have Spanish programming. They are doing quite well reaching that market, and they were helpful in relating their stories.

INTRODUCTION

The history of Oklahoma City radio is in many ways a history of broadcasting in America. And much of it is also the history of Oklahoma. In many ways, it mirrors the success and influence Oklahomans have had in many fields. We think of this as the Oklahoma spirit that those pioneers who founded this state had. They worked hard to be the best at what they did.

In 1920, an entrepreneur from upstate New York moved to Oklahoma City. Earl Hull was interested in this new invention called radio. Here, he met another man, H.S. Richards, who was also interested in this new invention. Both had built small radios early in their lives. Together they built a station, 5XT, and in January 1920, they put it on the air.

That station became WKY, went through several owners, and in 1928 was purchased by E.K. Gaylord, owner of the *Daily Oklahoman* newspaper.

Soon, another radio station went on the air. KFJF would eventually become KOMA. Muskogee grocery man John T. Griffin owned it through the mid-1950s. Both WKY, affiliated with the National Broadcasting Company (NBC), and KOMA, affiliated with the Columbia Broadcasting System (CBS), were sending regular daily programs from Oklahoma City to their networks in the 1940s and early 1950s. And both became launching pads for the careers of Curt Gowdy, Walter Cronkite, and Paul Harvey, among others. Oklahoma City radio quickly became a hotbed of talent.

In 1928, WKY was purchased by E.K. Gaylord, owner of the *Daily Oklahoman*, *Oklahoma City Times*, and *Oklahoma Farmer-Stockman* newspapers. Gaylord had worked hard to make his papers the best and had always hired good people when positions opened, then gave them the assets they needed to achieve excellence and provided them with encouragement. Now he did the same with the radio station, building a new transmitter plant with the latest equipment and moving the studios to a newly constructed building.

The same thing was happening at KFJF, now KOMA. It was purchased by grocery magnate John T. Griffin, who set out to actively compete with WKY. WKY was affiliated with NBC, and KOMA was a CBS affiliate. By the late 1930s, both were sending programs originating in Oklahoma City to their networks for broadcast nationally.

In 1958, KOMA was purchased by Todd Storz, the inventor of Top 40 rock and roll radio. WKY had advance notice of the pending sale and copied all the programming elements, promotions, and contests Storz was using at his stations in Kansas City, New Orleans, and Minneapolis. The delay by the FCC in transferring KOMA's license to Storz gave WKY a three-month jump on going to the Top 40 format using many of promotions, liners, and other elements of the format Storz was using in his other markets. That began one of the legendary battles in rock and roll radio.

In 1974, an enterprising broadcaster in Oklahoma City took a floundering FM station, began playing country-and-western music, and took KEBC to number one in the radio ratings in Oklahoma City. About the same time, a group of black radio pioneers began playing soul music on an AM-FM station and brought it to great success. The lead DJ, Big Ben Tipton, was elected to the Oklahoma City Council and enjoyed great success there. Another leader in the African American community, Russell Perry had been the quarterback on the football team at the all-black high school in Oklahoma City. In one of the first games played between a black high school and a white high school, he led his team to victory. In 1979, Perry started the *Black Chronicle* newspaper, and about the same time, purchased a daytime AM station and began Perry Publishing and Broadcasting Company. Today, his newspaper covers the black community statewide. He owns radio stations in Oklahoma City, Tulsa, and Lawton. He also served as the Oklahoma secretary of economic development and special affairs from May 2000 to May 2001.

Jack Ogle and Bob Barry Sr. became the voices of University of Oklahoma Sooner football in 1961. They had worked together at KNOR in Norman, Oklahoma, and were close friends. At the same time they began Sooner broadcasts, Ogle was hired as a newsman on WKY Radio. Within a year, he was moved to WKY-TV as a news anchor. Soon, Barry was hired as the weekend sports anchor at WKY-TV. In 1964, he was promoted to sports director, and worked there until his retirement in 2008. He was the voice of OU from 1961 to 1971, the University of Tulsa from 1972 to 1973, Oklahoma State University from 1973 to 1990, and back at the University of Oklahoma from 1991 to 2011. He is the only major university play-by-play announcer to have called games for 50 consecutive years, calling all three major universities in Oklahoma. His legacy continued when he stepped down as sports director in 1997 and his son Bob Barry Jr. took over. Barry Sr. continued doing the 6:00 p.m. sports until his full retirement in 2008. He died in 2011, and Bob Barry Jr. was killed in a traffic accident in 2015. Ogle had three sons—Kent and Kevin, who are news anchors at KFOR-TV (NBC, formerly WKY-TV), and Kelly, who anchors at KWTV (CBS). Kevin's daughter Abagail anchors at KOCO-TV (ABC), and her sister Katelyn is a reporter/producer with their uncle at KWTV (CBS).

One

IN THE BEGINNING

In 1920, radio as it is known today began in Oklahoma City. Earl Hull moved from New York to Oklahoma City in 1920. An Army veteran of the Great War, Hull had been interested in wireless communication while a student at St. Lawrence University in Canton, New York. He grew up in Niagara Falls, New York. In 1917, he joined the Army, wanting to be a flyer. Aviation was at the time a part of the Signal Corps, and the Signal Corps was based at Fort Sill, Oklahoma. It was there that Hull, already interested in wireless communication, really found that interest taking off.

Hull traveled to Oklahoma City and met H.S. Richards while there. Both had been bitten by the radio bug, and both built radio sets at early ages. Hull continued serving in the Army, organizing a radio unit and teaching electronics at Fort Sill.

As they recalled years later, in January 1920 they assembled enough parts to build a 20-watt transmitter in the garage of a home at 1011 West Ash Avenue, just west of the Oklahoma City Stock Yards and associated meatpacking plants in an area called Packingtown. Hull was living in the home with Richards and his family. If they kept any records of the dates of that early station, they were lost. Hull later recalled that they applied for an experimental license and were assigned the call letters 5XT. Two wooden poles held what was called a "flat top" antenna, which was strung over the roof of the modest home.

On January 1, 1922, the *Daily Oklahoman* published a survey of radio in Oklahoma City. It revealed there were 30 receivers and two transmitters in the city. One of the transmitters was only used for wireless telegraphy. The other was 5XT.

On February 21, 1922, Hull received a new license from the Department of Commerce, Bureau of Navigation, moving his station to 1040 Kcs, increasing the power to 200 watts and assigning new call letters. He was now the owner of WKY. At the same time, the *Daily Oklahoman* reported the station would begin a regular daily schedule of "nightly programs such as the one broadcast by Pittsburgh, Detroit and other large stations."

The other business Hull and Richards owned, the Oklahoma Radio Shop, was booming. When Richards traveled to the East Coast to buy tubes and other radio parts, he found the factories there could not keep up with demand. Ultimately, he and Hull announced the Oklahoma Radio Shop had been selected as a distributor for the Radio Corporation of America (RCA).

On Christmas Eve 1922, another radio station hit the airwaves with the arrival of KFJF. This station was owned by Dudley Shaw, an enterprising Oklahoma City businessman. It was described by the *Daily Oklahoman* as being located at 406 North Harvey Avenue in downtown Oklahoma City and was broadcasting phonograph music heard in several states: "Friday night the Centenary Methodist Church Orchestra and the Marshall and Harper ladies quartette will broadcast a program."

E.K. Gaylord had arrived in Oklahoma City between Christmas and New Year's Eve 1902. He was hired by the owner of the *Daily Oklahoman* as business manager. At about the same time, an advertising agency executive in New York created a new kind of advertisement business. Rather than sell companies advertising, George Katz began the reverse, representing newspapers to get the agencies to buy advertisements for their clients in the papers he represented. Gaylord and the *Daily Oklahoman* became one of Katz's first clients.

In 1916, the owner of the *Daily Oklahoman* decided to sell the newspaper to Gaylord, but Gaylord needed financing. Katz came to the rescue and became part owner of the paper.

WKY went through several ownership changes, culminating with H.W. Duncan selling the station in May 1928 to Harrison Smith. In July 1928, Harrison Smith called Walter Harrison and told him he wanted to sell WKY to the *Daily Oklahoman* or he "would give the damn thing to Scripps-Howard," owner of a daily newspaper that competed against the *Daily Oklahoman*. Later that day, Walter Harrison spoke with Burdette Blue, vice president and general manager of the Indian Territory Illuminating Oil Company. The company was drilling a test well on the southeast side of Oklahoma City. Blue told Harrison the discovery well would be big and there would be an Oklahoma City oil field.

Harrison and Edgar Bell sent a cablegram to Gaylord and his wife, who were vacationing in Paris, telling him about the offer and threat and that Blue told them an "oil field in Oklahoma City is definite." Gaylord cabled back his okay to buy the station. In December, the well hit oil and gushed for seven days. The Oklahoma City oil field became the most productive field ever discovered in Oklahoma.

In 1928, when Gaylord bought WKY, the radio station became Katz's first radio client. That would have a major effect on radio in Oklahoma City in 1958.

Gaylord had already developed a reputation for excellence with his newspapers. Now he turned his attention to doing the same thing with his newly purchased radio station. The station had dilapidated, poorly equipped studios in the basement of the Huckins Hotel, so Gaylord rented the second floor of the just completed Plaza Court Building and began construction of a new modern transmitting plant west of Oklahoma City.

The same thing was happening at KFJF, Now KOMA, which was purchased by grocery magnate John T. Griffin, who set out to compete with WKY. By the late 1930s, both stations were sending local programs to their networks for broadcast nationally.

Pictured is a formal portrait of Earl Hull in which he is identified as the WKY engineer. Hull built and maintained the equipment from its conception through the early 1930s. After E.K. Gaylord hired an engineer, Hull left Oklahoma and moved to Niagara Falls, New York, where he owned the local station until his death in May 1971. There are no known photographs of H.S. Richards.

The garage of H.S. Richards's house at 1011 West Ash Avenue became the home of 5XT; Earl Hull designed and built the broadcasting equipment, including a phonograph player and other gear necessary to broadcast voice and music.

13

The living room of the Richards home served as their studio. An entire church choir was jammed into this living room for an Easter broadcast in 1922. This room was also used for speeches, plays, and live musical programs WKY broadcast. The home is often described as Earl Hull's house, but in fact, it was the home of H.S. Richards and his family, and Hull lived there as a boarder.

Earl Hull continued to look for new ways to promote radio. In the summer of 1922, the Oklahoma National Guard commissioned him a lieutenant, and he immediately announced the formation of a special radio unit. Hull had served in the Army Signal Corps during World War I, which led to his interest in electronics. The Signal Corps was based at Fort Sill, near Lawton, Oklahoma. It was only natural the Oklahoma National Guard would offer him a commission to teach the new field of radio electronics at Fort Sill.

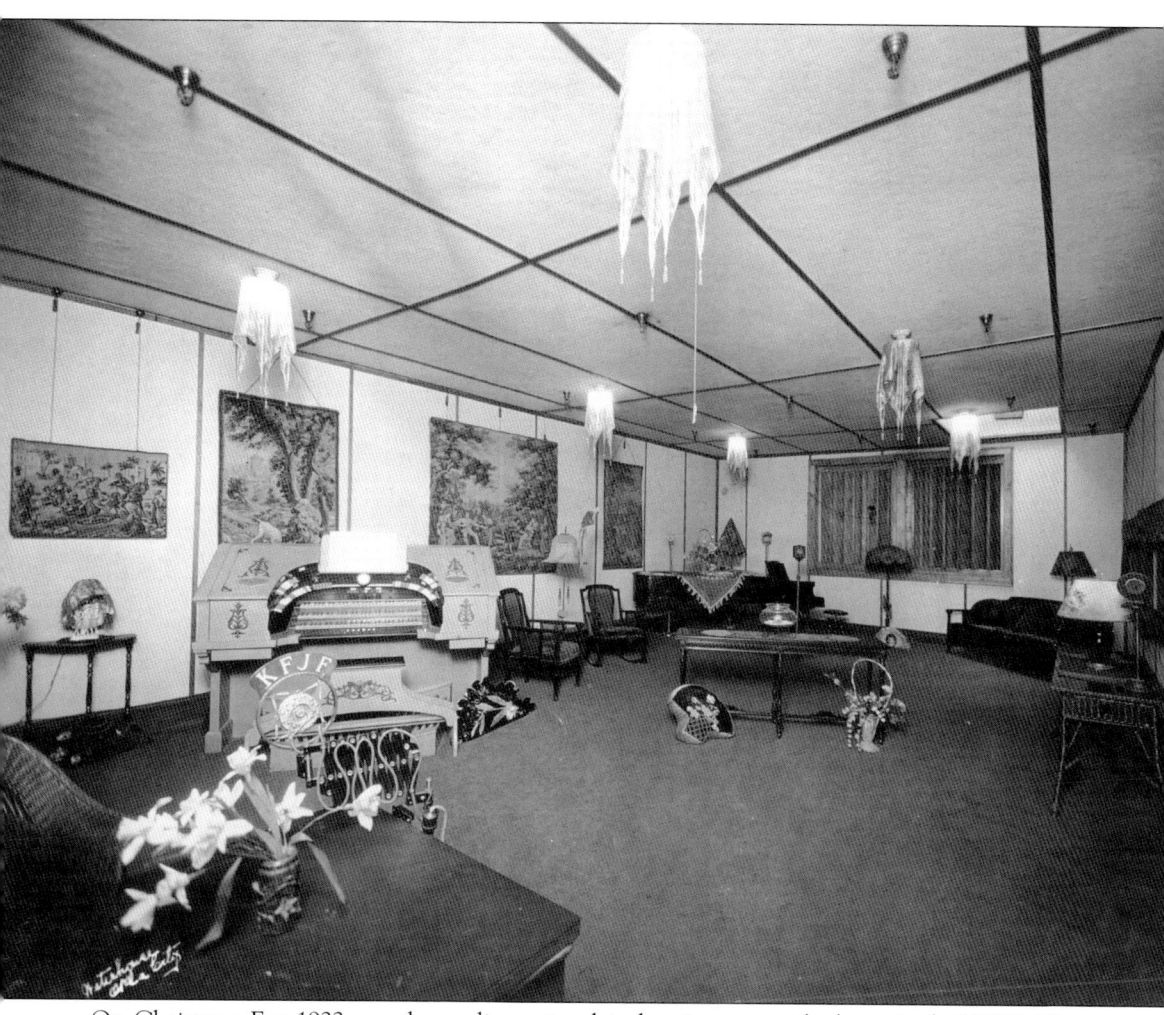

On Christmas Eve 1922, another radio station hit the airwaves with the arrival of KFJF. This station was owned by Dudley Shaw, an enterprising Oklahoma City businessman. As was the case with many, if not all, stations in the early 1920s, there are conflicting stories. One is that KFJF was not licensed until July 1923. The original license was issued to the National Radio Manufacturing Company (owned by Shaw), which had been involved in another station in 1922 that was never licensed. This new station was described by the *Daily Oklahoman* as being located at 406 North Harvey Avenue in downtown Oklahoma City, but it was soon moved to this "living room" studio in the Security Building, which was also downtown. Many stations designed their studios to appear like living rooms to place the performers in more comfortable surroundings and help them feel at ease.

Radio Station (WKY) studio in the Huckins hotel   Huckins
1924-28

By 1926, stations had begun selling advertising, but it would take several years before any station began showing a profit. Hull and Richards began trying to sell WKY. They had moved to new studios in the basement of the Huckins Hotel in the heart of downtown. The Huckins Hotel, in 1910, became the temporary state capitol when voters across the state approved moving the capital from Guthrie to Oklahoma City. It took several years for the state government to decide where to locate the capitol building, buy the land, and construct it. For years, hotels in downtown Oklahoma City continued to be home to two radio stations.

In September, Hull and Richards found a buyer. A five-man group of businessmen led by H.W. Duncan bought the station. They retained Hull as the engineer because he had built most of the equipment and was the only one who knew how to run it and maintain it. The five partners were in constant disagreement on how to operate the station. Duncan sued two of the partners and bought out the other two to become the sole owner of WKY. As with many other owners, he was also an announcer on the station, known as "The Cheery Old Skipper."

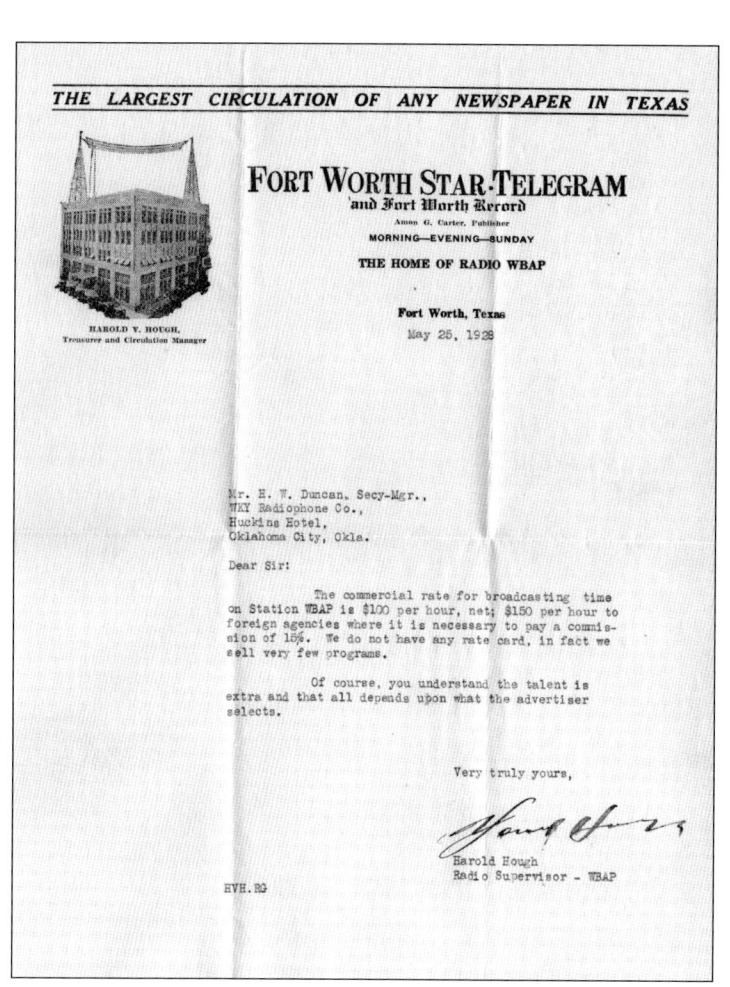

> **THE LARGEST CIRCULATION OF ANY NEWSPAPER IN TEXAS**
>
> **FORT WORTH STAR-TELEGRAM**
> and Fort Worth Record
> Amon G. Carter, Publisher
> MORNING—EVENING—SUNDAY
>
> THE HOME OF RADIO WBAP
>
> Fort Worth, Texas
> May 25, 1928
>
> HAROLD V. HOUGH,
> Treasurer and Circulation Manager
>
> Mr. E. W. Duncan, Secy-Mgr.,
> WKY Radiophone Co.,
> Huckins Hotel,
> Oklahoma City, Okla.
>
> Dear Sir:
>
> The commercial rate for broadcasting time on Station WBAP is $100 per hour, net; $150 per hour to foreign agencies where it is necessary to pay a commission of 15%. We do not have any rate card, in fact we sell very few programs.
>
> Of course, you understand the talent is extra and that all depends upon what the advertiser selects.
>
> Very truly yours,
>
> Harold Hough
> Radio Supervisor - WBAP
>
> HVH.RG

Advertising sales continued to lag, and in 1928, Duncan sent letters to a number of radio stations in the region asking them how they were selling time and what they were charging. The letters went to stations such as KVOO Tulsa, WBAP Fort Worth, and KTHS Hot Springs, Arkansas. This letter from WBAP indicates the sale of airtime was slow even in Fort Worth.

RATE SCALE
COMMERCIAL PROGRAMS OVER STATION WKY

	OPEN RATE	WKLY 3 MO.	WKLY 6 MO.	WKLY 9 MO.	WKLY 1 YR.
1 Hour	$60.00	$55.00	$50.00	$45.00	$40.00
1/2 "	35.00	32.50	30.00	27.50	25.00
1/4 "	20.00	18.75	17.50	16.25	15.00
2 Hours	100.00	90.00	80.00	70.00	60.00

Using an index card, Duncan typed this rate scale, as he called it—the first one for WKY.

For several years, Walter Harrison, managing editor of the *Daily Oklahoman*, and Edgar Bell, business manager of the paper, had been trying to persuade E.K. Gaylord, owner of the *Daily Oklahoman*, to buy WKY. This letter shows the agreement by which the *Daily Oklahoman* referred to WKY as its broadcasting station even before the newspaper purchased it. Many newspapers had obtained early radio licenses in their markets, even though radio was not profitable. Hull had attempted to sell WKY to Gaylord, but Gaylord refused, saying there were a lot of bugs in radio and a lot of money to be lost as well. The year 1928 was a year that Oklahoma history would forever remember and a year that would change the radio industry in Oklahoma City. That spring, the Indian Territory Illuminating Oil Company (ITIO, later City Service Oil and Gas Company) began a discovery oil well in southeast Oklahoma City.

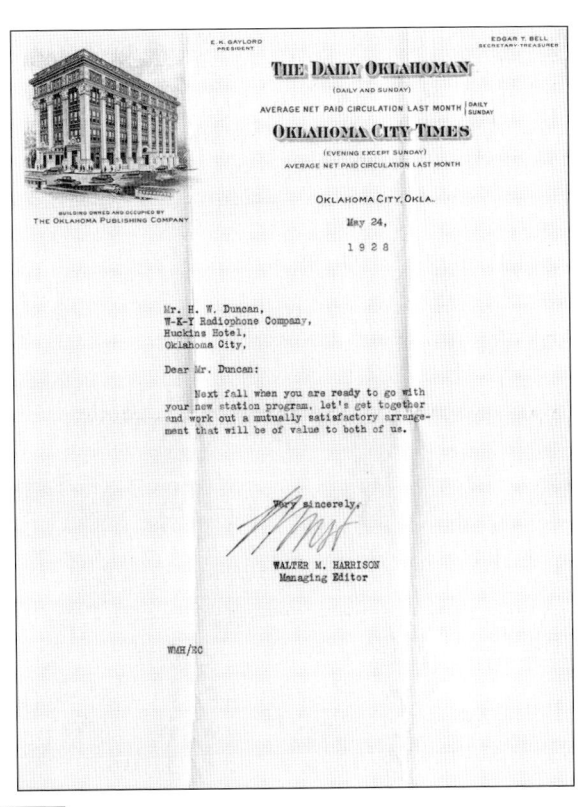

E.K. Gaylord came to Oklahoma City around Christmas 1902 and became business manager of the *Daily Oklahoman*. In 1916, he bought controlling interest in the newspaper and established it as the most influential newspaper in the state.

19

In May 1928, Duncan, who had purchased WKY from Hull for $7,500, sold the station to Harrison Smith, who owned the Atwater Kent Radio distributorship for Oklahoma and North Texas. It was one of the best-selling radios at that time. In July, Smith sold the station to Gaylord for $5,000. Finally, WKY had stable ownership and the means to become a great radio station. Within days of the sale, the *Daily Oklahoman* began running a number of stories about the station, its creation, and its plans for it. Shortly before the sale, the previous owner announced plans to buy and install a 1,000-watt Western Electric transmitter to replace the original 150-watt transmitter Earl Hull had built in 1921.

The new owners also announced they had leased the entire second floor of the Plaza Court building, just completed by prominent developer and dentist G.A. Nichols. The new offices and studios were state-of-the-art in the new building at Tenth Street and Walker Avenue, just north of Classen's Highland Park addition or what is now known as Heritage Hills. These unidentified singers are performing in the new studio. The hope was that with new ownership, studios, and a higher-powered transmitter, WKY would be able to join one of the new national chains or networks. And with AT&T Long Lines Division about to complete a new high-capacity set of long lines that would eventually connect Chicago to San Antonio and Houston with the capability to carry broadcast-quality signals, that seemed a possibility.

#32
WKY radio transmitted its signal from this complex during the 1930s. (Courtesy Archives & Manuscripts Division of the Oklahoma Historical Society.)

The new transmitter had not been delivered, so land was purchased west of Oklahoma City for the new WKY transmission plant. The location was described in the paper as being "seven miles northwest of Oklahoma City on the 39th Street highway."

The new 1,000-watt Western Electric transmitter was installed and was now on the air. This was state-of-the-art broadcasting that E.K. Gaylord, owner of the *Daily Oklahoman* and now WKY would continue until the end of his life. Within a month of moving into the new studios and putting the new transmitter on the air, on December 21, 1928, WKY began carrying programs from NBC. That began a relationship between WKY and NBC that continued through the 1970s.

Two

WKY and KOMA Become Big-Time Radio Stations

Soon after the government approved the transfer of WKY's license to Oklahoma Publishing Company, E.K. Gaylord began looking for a "radio man" to manage the station. He found him in Omaha, Nebraska. Gayle Grubb was known on the air as "Gloomy Gus." He knew radio, management, sales, and announcing. Earl Hull stayed on as an engineer and eventually also became an announcer.

Meanwhile, over in the Security Building, KFJF continued to have problems. Inspections by the Federal Radio Commission revealed the transmitter was frequently drifting off its assigned frequency, the station was deeply in debt, and a new owner was taking over. After years of struggling with KFJF, Dudley Shaw decided to retire. Southwestern Broadcasting Company was the new owner and promptly changed the call letters to KOMA. Soon, the station was sold again, this time to Hearst Radio, a division of Hearst Publishing.

Sports broadcasting, and specifically University of Oklahoma football, became important. In the summer of 1937, WKY began looking for someone who could announce OU football games. Gayle Grubb found 20-year-old Walter Cronkite Jr. working at KCMO in Kansas City recreating football games using Western Union sports bulletins. Cronkite had never broadcast a live football game. He had been a campus reporter for Scripps-Howard and read scores on a local radio station while a student at the University of Texas from 1933 to 1935. After a short time in Houston as a cub reporter with a newspaper there, he moved to Kansas City.

After being hired by WKY, he built a spotting board with lights to indicate various players. He hired a couple of spotters to flip the switches on the light board.

Cronkite's first game was OU at Tulsa, with the Sooners loosing 19 to 7 at Skelly Stadium. Grubb was in the booth with Cronkite and after the game asked him what he thought. Cronkite responded, "It was terrible." One problem was the light board did not work. He told Grubb he was going to throw it away. For the next game, Cronkite and Perry Ward, who was the color analyst, memorized the rosters, names, numbers, and hometowns of the players on both teams.

Monday morning at 6:30, Grubb and Cronkite were called into E.K. Gaylord's office, who told them he thought the broadcast went pretty well. Cronkite thought the rest of the season went, in his words, "marvelous."

After football season was over, Cronkite was assigned to the WKY news department and began working as a journalist. Years later, he told many people he credited his career at CBS to the news he had done at WKY Radio.

In 1945, KOMA was broadcasting the OU football games. In August, general manager Ken Brown took his family on vacation to Yellowstone National Park. Driving through Wyoming, they stopped in Cheyenne, where they heard a young man calling a baseball game on a local radio station. Brown was impressed with what he heard and called the station to find out how to reach the young announcer he had heard. The next morning, he called the young man and told him he thought he might be looking for a play-by-play announcer that fall and wondered if he would be interested in working at KOMA and calling OU football games.

The young man was astonished. "My gosh," he thought. "The 50,000-watt CBS station carrying Oklahoma University football games?"

He told Brown he certainly was interested. Brown told him he would be in touch. That summer the opening occurred, and Brown called the young man, Curt Gowdy, and told him to pack his bag and get himself to Oklahoma City.

Gowdy arrived in time to call the first three seasons of Bud Wilkinson–coached OU football games. He also called Oklahoma A&M (now Oklahoma State University) basketball games and Oklahoma City's Texas League baseball games. In 1948, Red Barber at CBS Sports called Gowdy to tell him CBS was going to carry his call of the Oklahoma football game with Texas Christian University. Gowdy was stunned and nervous. After the broadcast he said, "I managed to forget that this was coast-to-coast over CBS and worked as if it were just another Oklahoma football game over station KOMA."

At the end of the 1948 baseball season, broadcaster Russ Hodges left the New York Yankees for the New York Giants. The Yankees needed a replacement to be the number two man behind Mel Allen. Allen and Gowdy had met the previous winter when the Oklahoma A&M basketball team was playing a game in New York City. Gowdy was urged to apply for the Yankees job, and three weeks later, was hired. He began at the start of the 1949 baseball season.

Gene Autry was born in a small town in North Texas. While he was young, his parents moved to a small town in south-central Oklahoma. After he left high school in 1925, he became a telegraph operator for the St. Louis–San Francisco Railroad, working at the train station in Chelsea, Oklahoma, just east of Tulsa. One night, a man came into the station while Autry was playing his guitar and singing to himself. The man told Autry he ought to be singing on the radio. When Autry looked up, he recognized Will Rogers was speaking to him. Soon, Autry was singing on the radio, first on KVOO Tulsa, then in the movies and on CBS Radio.

As Autry became increasingly successful, he built a horse ranch near Ardmore, Oklahoma. On November 16, 1941, the town of Berwyn, Oklahoma, north of Ardmore, was renamed in his honor. The ceremony was broadcast live on CBS by KOMA.

Beginning in 1939, WKY began feeding a number of regular weekly programs to the NBC network. On January 21, 1939, *Southwestern Stars* debuted on the NBC Blue network, then a few weeks later switched to the NBC Red network. Soon, more WKY programs were appearing on the Red network, including *Cameos of Melody*, *Southwestern Serenade*, *Campfire Embers*, and *Southern Rivers*. Then on November 14, 1941, *Dark Fantasy* premiered. The Friday night horror show was described as weird, creepy, exciting, and mysterious. The show ran for more than a year on NBC. And over at KOMA, they were also producing programs for CBS, including a Thursday night series of dramas written by the Oklahoma section of the Federal Writers Project. The scripts included many subjects of Oklahoma history, including the Trail of Tears and the story of two freed slaves who wrote spirituals, including "Swing Low, Sweet Chariot."

THE HOME OF KOMA
ATOP THE BILTMORE HOTEL

Filling the entire twenty-fourth floor of the Biltmore Hotel in Oklahoma City are the studios and offices of KOMA. Here, amid modern, air-conditioned surroundings, originate KOMA's features.

The Reception Lobby, showing the window into studio "A" at the left, and corridor to studio "B", right.

Studio "B", designed primarily for "talk" programs, or small instrumental features.

Studio "A", KOMA's setting for variety and most musical presentations.

The Audition Lounge, where clients or staff may review a program in "dress rehearsal" without its being broadcast.

The Civic Room of the Biltmore Hotel is frequently used as a KOMA studio when audience space is required.

KOMA

The bright spot for KOMA was affiliating with CBS in January 1929, about a month after WKY gained its network affiliation with NBC. The new owner leased the 24th floor at the top of the newly completed Biltmore Hotel and moved the studios and offices there. The transmitter was northwest of Oklahoma City, near Edmond.

On November 19, 1930, a tornado struck the Oklahoma City suburb of Bethany, killing 23 people and leaving hundreds injured or homeless. The Red Cross sent an appeal for $30,000 to help the victims. Oklahoma Publishing Company business manager Edgar Bell and WKY manager Gayle Grubb went on the air with the appeal.

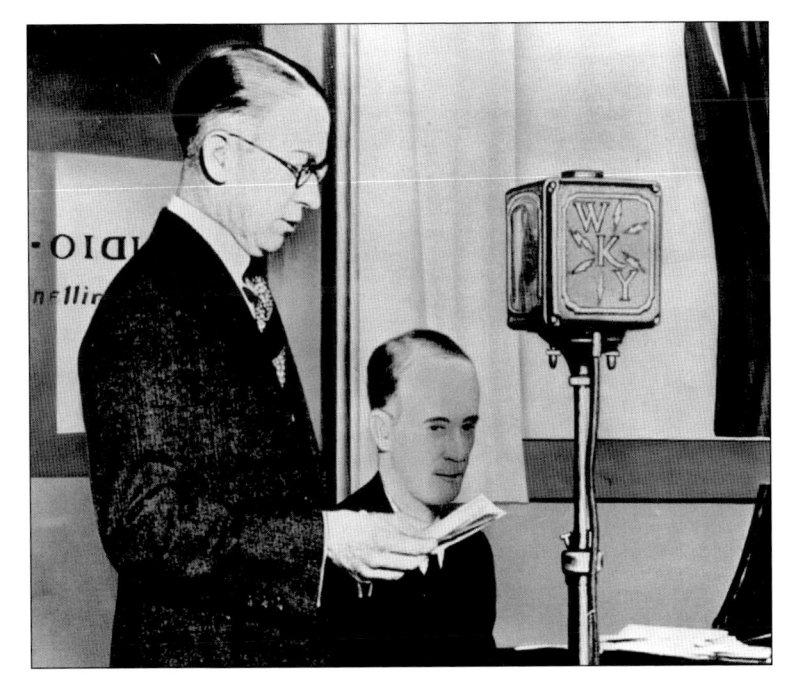

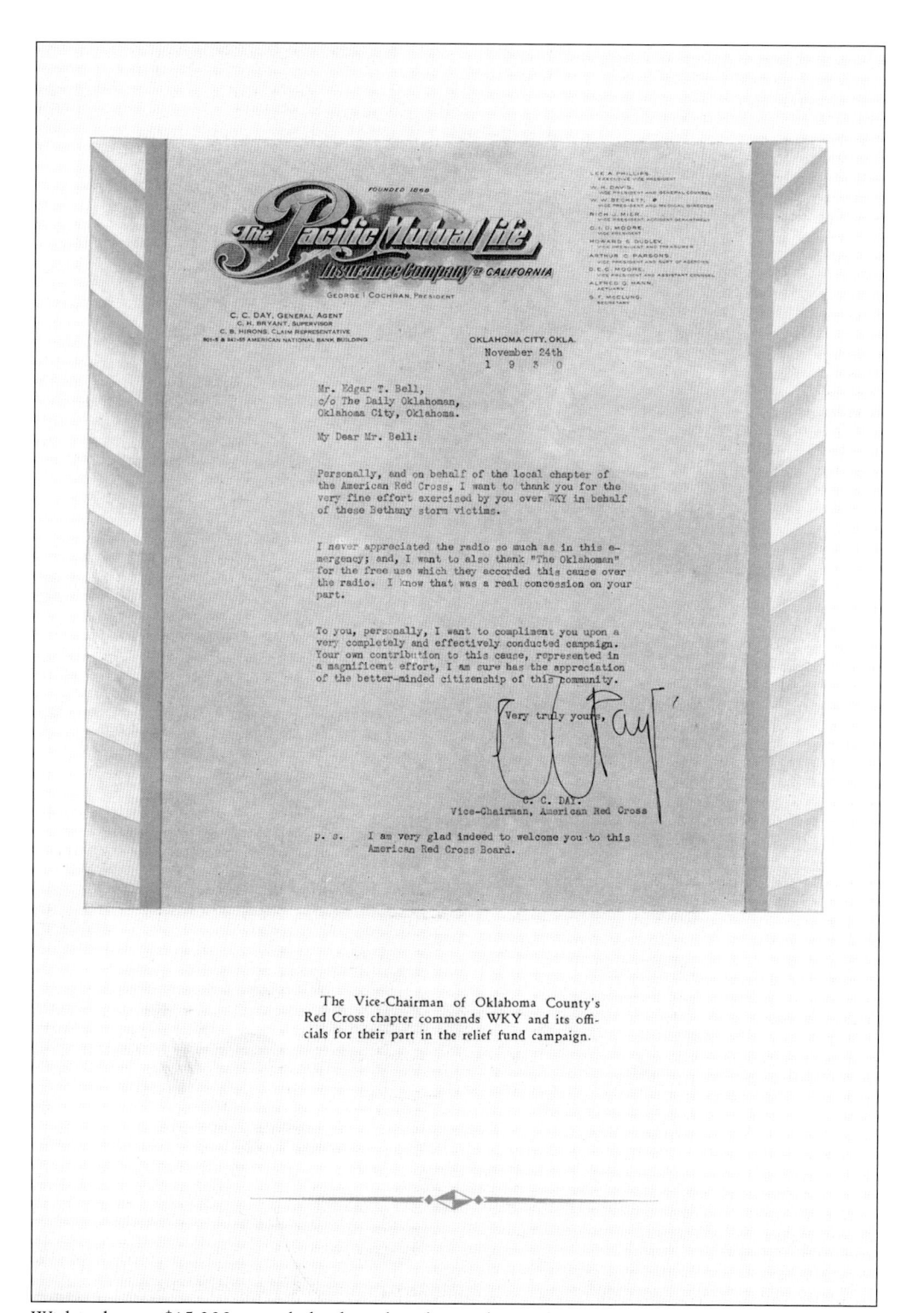

> The Vice-Chairman of Oklahoma County's Red Cross chapter commends WKY and its officials for their part in the relief fund campaign.

Within hours, $15,000 was pledged, and within a day and a half, the Red Cross had exceeded its goal.

Over the years and more so in the television era, WKY Radio and TV became training grounds for many newscasters, announcers, and even management personnel who landed at NBC. These three WKY announcers are visiting the NBC studios in Los Angeles. From left to right are Bob Latting, Daryl McAllister, and Perry Ward. All three announced programs that were broadcast on NBC. In addition, Ward left WKY for KOMA, where he was the announcer for the *Gene Autry's Melody Ranch* program on CBS.

Among the new pieces of equipment from RCA that were installed at WKY were the first directional microphones and shortwave transmitters used for remote broadcasts.

In 1935, Count G. Mazzaglia Cutelli was brought to the WKY studios to install the latest sound-making equipment. An Italian immigrant, the count had appeared in vaudeville and gained a reputation for creating sound effects. Walt Disney employed him to voice Mickey Mouse, and he was also the voice of Porky Pig. Both NBC and Hollywood used him to create sound effects for various programs and movies.

In late 1935, William Skirvin completed construction of the Skirvin Plaza building across the street from his Skirvin Hotel. Gaylord leased the entire fifth floor for studios and offices for WKY.

RCA engineers were brought in to install the newest RCA broadcast equipment. They had recently completed the RCA Building in Manhattan and Radio City Music Hall.

On April 1, 1935, the first broadcasts were originated from the new studios. A dinner for 700 invited guests was served before the live programs began in Main Studio A. On April 13, the studios were formally dedicated. They were described as modern with the latest equipment and were comparable to the NBC studios in New York and Los Angeles.

There were even two kitchen studios for *Daily Oklahoman* food columnist Aunt Susan, who presented a cooking show each morning.

One kitchen studio was equipped with a gas range, while the other featured an electric one.

Main Studio A featured a Kilgen theater organ that cost $33,000 to purchase and install. The organ used 1,192 pipes to create its sounds. Theater organs had mainly been used in movie theaters to add music to silent films. On April 13, 1936, Jessie Crawford, the "Poet of the Organ" and organist at NBC in New York, came to Oklahoma City to give the premier performance on WKY's Kilgen.

A week later, WKY hired Ken Wright to move to Oklahoma City from the NBC station in Chicago. At 10:45 every night, he presented an hour of music on the grand organ. Wright remained part of the WKY staff, playing various organs through the 1970s.

Another national broadcast from WKY on NBC took place in 1936, from October 17 to October 24, when the Twin Hills Golf Course in Oklahoma City hosted the annual PGA championship. It took 35 people from WKY to produce the broadcasts. They built five wooden towers around the course so the announcers could see the action from various vantage points. Shown here is Gayle Grubb broadcasting from a tower. Along with Grubb, Edgar Bell and *Daily Oklahoman* managing editor Walter Harrison were part of the announcing crew.

On January 21, 1939, WKY began originating network programs for NBC with the broadcast of *Southwestern Stars*. Following that show were *Cameos of Melody*, *Southwestern Serenade*, *Summertime Swing*, *Campfire Embers*, and *Southern Rivers*. This is the cast of the *Anthony Avenues* program.

Popular Oklahoma City singer Helen Webb was a regular on several of the programs WKY broadcast locally and on the NBC network, as were country singer Jimmy Wakely of Rosedale, Oklahoma (left), and Johnny Bond of Marietta, Oklahoma (right), both of whom found national success as singers and songwriters after many appearances on WKY.

Another frequent provider of music was the Al Good Orchestra, shown here performing in the grand ballroom at the Skirvin Hotel. Soon after emigrating from Sweden, Good was hired by WKY as a staff musician. He soon formed the orchestra, which appeared frequently on WKY programs and on certain programs broadcast on NBC. The orchestra still plays today.

In 1941, WKY began producing a weekly horror drama called *Dark Fantasy* for NBC. The show ran on Friday nights, live from the WKY studios at 12:30 a.m. Eastern time. It premiered on November 14, 1941. Here, one of the actors is rehearsing his lines before a broadcast.

In 1938, Oklahoma ownership returned to KOMA, when Muskogee businessman J.T. Griffin bought the station. Griffin was a cofounder of Griffin Foods in Muskogee and had entered the radio business in 1932 with the purchase of KTUL radio in Tulsa. He wanted to make KOMA comparable to WKY in delivering network quality programs to Oklahoma City listeners and CBS.

America's entrance into World War II meant the construction of the Army Air Corps Midwest Air Depot, a large maintenance base and adjoining Douglas Aircraft factory on the east side of Oklahoma City. The presence of the Army Air Corps brought war bond drives, which meant Hollywood stars were coming to Oklahoma City. In 1944, WKY broadcast this appearance by Bob Hope during one those drives. The facility was renamed Turner Air Force Base after the war.

By 1945, KOMA was producing *Oklahoma Roundup*, featuring Oklahoma western bands weekday afternoons at 6:45 p.m. Eastern time on the CBS network. Griffin had hired Perry Ward away from WKY, and he was the announcer on *Oklahoma Roundup*. Ward was also the announcer for a time in 1948 on the CBS western *Gene Autry's Melody Ranch*. By late 1945, after World War II, KOMA had an advantage over WKY when it became a 50,000-watt clear channel station. This meant that the station's nighttime signal covered all of the western half of the United States.

Earl Sinclair is pictured checking the Associated Press teletypes for the latest war news. The WKY newsroom featured much the same equipment as the NBC newsrooms. On the evening of June 6, 1944, the news was filled with reports from London on the D-Day invasion of Normandy. NBC ran a special program featuring live reports on local reactions to news of the invasion from affiliates across the country, ending with WKY. Dow Mooney told the radio audience that "Oklahoma's Sunday school–teaching governor, Robert S. Kerr, led the state in praying for our servicemen and their success in the landing."

In 1937, Gayle Grubb thought it might be a good idea to broadcast University of Oklahoma football games. Walter Cronkite was a sportswriter who was hired by KCMO in Kansas City as an announcer. Cronkite is shown second from left on Owen Field interviewing halfback Beryl Clark. Head football coach Tom Stidham has his back to the camera at far right.

After Cronkite left WKY, Jack Shafer was hired to broadcast OU football games. Here, he is interviewing OU athletic director Jack Haskell before the 1940 season got under way. Haskell served in the Navy during World War II but returned after the war to resume his duties.

Curt broadcasts one of his twice-daily series of sports programs.

Jerry Marx, one of Oklahoma's most listened-to newscasters.

Edward R. Murrow

Ben Holmes covers the local news front, compiles and edits the news gathered by the world wide facilities of United Press.

Bill Henry

Lowell Thomas

In 1945, Ken Brown, general manager of KOMA, and his family were traveling to Jackson, Wyoming, on vacation. They stopped in Cheyenne to spend the night. Brown was listening to a baseball game on a local radio station and was impressed with the play-by-play announcer. He called the station and was given the announcer's name and phone number and told he was living with his parents. The next morning, Brown spoke with the young man and told him that KOMA was probably going to need a play-by-play announcer soon. A few months later, the opening occurred, and he called the young man back to see if he was interested in moving to Oklahoma City. Curt Gowdy was thrilled to be offered the job of play-by-play announcer for the OU Sooners, now led by Bud Wilkinson, on the giant 50,000-watt CBS affiliate in Oklahoma City. He accepted the job and gleefully headed south to the Sooner State. While at KOMA, Gowdy also did play-by-play of Oklahoma City's Texas League baseball team, the Oklahoma City Indians. During the 1948 basketball season, Oklahoma A&M played a game in New York. Gowdy met Mel Allen there. Later, when the Yankees were looking for a number two man to help Allen, they remembered meeting Gowdy. He was interviewed for the job. In 1949, Curt Gowdy became the number two announcer for the New York Yankees.

Three

ONE OF AMERICA'S BIGGEST ROCK 'N' ROLL RADIO BATTLES

By the mid-1950s, radio was changing, both locally and nationally. Television was becoming the medium of choice for many Americans. And Oklahoma City had become the frontlines in these changes. Music played by disk jockeys replaced programs. Various music formats were coming to the forefront. Country-and-western music and soul music were becoming popular. Stations were running contests giving away prizes and money. Many popular radio programs such as *The Lone Ranger*, *Dragnet*, and big band shows moved from radio to television.

In 1953, Omaha broadcaster Todd Storz bought a station in New Orleans, WTIX, and invented the Top 40 format. A year later, he bought a station in Kansas City, WHB, and installed his rock and roll format there. WHB became the highest-rated station in Kansas City. In 1958, Storz began the process of purchasing KOMA, but the Federal Communications Commission (FCC) took months to approve the sale. Meanwhile, George Katz, who was a partner in the *Daily Oklahoman* and WKY Radio and who represented WKY with national advertisers, hired the program director from WHB to be his "radio programming consultant." His first assignment was to go to Oklahoma City and advise his client, radio station WKY, of the changes they would need to make in advance of Storz's takeover of KOMA.

WKY sent staff to each of the markets where Storz owned stations, took voluminous notes, and put the Storz rock-and-roll format on the air at WKY.

Storz always promoted people from within his organization. As he was awaiting FCC approval for the sale, he promoted Jack Sampson from sales manager at WHB to general manager of KOMA. He also promoted DJ Rod Roddy, from his New Orleans station WTIX, to be program director at KOMA.

Months went by, and there was still no approval from the FCC on the license transfer. Sampson and Roddy were whiling away their time waiting to take over the 50,000-watt giant and listening to WKY broadcast all the Storz-type promotions, contests, and other programming elements in the Top 40 format. WKY had dropped its longtime affiliation with NBC. When Storz finally took control of KOMA, it would become the NBC affiliate in Oklahoma City. But the wait continued.

Rod Roddy began hiring DJs for the station but could not give them a start date because he did not know when the FCC would make a decision.

Meanwhile, Danny Williams, the program director at WKY, was hiring DJs as fast as he could. Among them was Don Wallace, who played the first rock-and-roll records on a Tulsa station and was booking sock hops, or dance parties, as fast as he could. He brought the sock hop rage to Oklahoma City and WKY. Ronny Kaye was working at a Lawton radio station when he received a call one Saturday afternoon. It was Danny Williams, who asked Kaye to meet him at his home Sunday afternoon for a job interview. The interview went well, and Kaye joined WKY.

Most of the original WKY disk jockeys were Oklahomans or were working in Oklahoma. Local news remained a big part of WKY Radio. The newscasters from the combined WKY Radio and TV news operation covered everything happening in and around central Oklahoma. And they became as well known as disk jockeys.

Finally, at Thanksgiving 1958, the FCC approved the sale. A large banquet was held in the Skirvin Hotel ballroom with hundreds of local businessmen and community leaders invited. NBC Radio set up a remote broadcast and aired a network newscast from the event. The mayor of Oklahoma City delivered a warm welcome to Todd Storz, his wife, and his corporate officers.

But Sampson and Roddy faced a problem. What would they do now that they actually had a station to run? Sampson uttered two words: "chicken rock." For the first three months, KOMA aired news from NBC and played a lot of Perry Como, Frank Sinatra, and other similar artists. Finally, Storz visited the station and told Sampson and Roddy to go rock and roll. He told them to find new ways to do the Top 40 format, since WKY had been using Storz's promotions for over three months.

The battle began. WKY had the full support of WKY-TV and the *Daily Oklahoman*. KOMA had a 50,000-watt signal on a clear channel at night that covered all of the central and western United States. WKY was number one in Oklahoma; KOMA was number one at night in cities such as Wichita, Amarillo, Santa Fe, Denver, and Lubbock and even into California. At night, there were just a handful of stations playing rock and roll that could be heard in rural America. These included WLS 890 Chicago, KAAY 1090 Little Rock, WNOE 1060 New Orleans, and others. But most teens in the Midwest waited for sundown to listen to KOMA 1520.

Through the 1960s, program director Rod Roddy was followed by Dean Johnson, Dale Wehba, and Perry Murphy. Disk jockeys including Charlie Tuna, Dale Wehba, Don McGregor, Paul Miller, John David, Chuck Dann, J. Michael Wilson, Johnny Dark, Buddy Scott, and John Ravencroft, among others, worked at KOMA.

The "Yours Truly, K-O-M-A" jingles from the PAMS jingle company in Dallas and the KOMA "Kissing Tone" set the station apart from the competition and created long-lasting memories.

When Storz purchased KOMA, the studio was located in the Terminal Building in downtown Oklahoma City, and the transmitter and three towers were in Moore, a small town just south of the city. Storz moved the studios and offices to the Moore transmitter site. Storz was an engineer at heart. He designed and built a reverb unit that was used on the studio microphones, using parts from a Hammond organ to create the effect. He also built one of the first automation units, and for about a year, KOMA was automated. However, that seemed to remove some of the personality of the DJs, so it was taken off the air.

Many of the WKY disk jockeys had programs on WKY-TV for cross promotion. Don Wallace had the hunting and fishing show *Wallace Wildlife*; Ronny Kaye had *The Scene*, a Saturday knockoff of *American Bandstand*; and Danny Williams had *3-D Danny*, an afternoon kids' show, and *Danny's Day*, a midday interview show. The other DJs appeared on these shows.

News was as important for KOMA as it was for WKY. KOMA newsmen won a number of state and regional awards and were keeping up with the large WKY news operation.

In the late 1970s, more changes in radio ended the battle. KOMA went country, and WKY went through several major format changes. The battle was over.

In late 1945, Gayle Grubb resigned as general manager of WKY to move to Los Angeles, where he became a vice president in a west coast broadcast ownership group. E.K. Gaylord looked to the Navy for his replacement, and in Corpus Christi, Texas, he found who he was looking for. Navy captain P.A. "Buddy" Sugg had been commanding the Naval Air Technical Center at the end of the war. Sugg held a master's degree in electrical engineering from the Massachusetts Institute of Technology and was the Navy's expert in the development of radar and sonar. This proved to be one of E.K. Gaylord's greatest hires. When in 1948 Gaylord decided to apply for one of the new television licenses, Buddy Sugg knew more about the technical side of television than the engineers working at WKY.

Buddy Sugg had a particular interest in advancing the equipment available for WKY Radio. In 1947, he told his engineers he wanted a portable radio station that could broadcast from events around the state. WKY purchased a 29-passenger bus from the Flexible Company and began equipping it. In May 1949, it was rolled out and began broadcasting. It was equipped with a gasoline generator, a complete control room, and a sound-treated studio large enough for nine people.

The studio at the rear of the bus had microphone connections for as many as nine people. No loud noises from outside the bus could be heard or picked up on the microphones.

Pictured is some of the equipment in the control room of the WKY Mobile Unit. All the equipment in the control room was shock mounted, enabling it to operate while the vehicle was in motion. The unit included the latest Bell Highway phones, where service was available. This enabled it to maintain contact with WKY master control. There were four AM-FM cue and talk back receivers, a 150-watt AM transmitter, turntables, and recorders.

By 1947, stations were replacing some of their daytime programs by playing records. Pictured is Bob Olson, WKY's "Platter Jockey." Many on the staff were not fond of this practice because it meant fewer jobs for actors and studio musicians.

On November 20, 1958, the FCC approved the transfer of KOMA's license to the inventor of Top 40 radio, Todd Storz. The next night he hosted a large banquet at the Skirvin Hotel to celebrate his ownership of KOMA. Standing and speaking at the banquet is George W. Armstrong, his partner in Midcontinent Broadcasting. Seated are, from left to right, Storz's attorney, Fred Berthelson; Storz's wife, Elizabeth, in a rare appearance; and Storz. Jack Sampson, sales manager at WHB, moved to Oklahoma City as general manager. A disk jockey from his New Orleans station WTIX, Rod Roddy, moved to Oklahoma City as program director. But they were in a quandary. WKY had been copying everything KOMA had planned to do for almost six months.

49

At the entrance to the banquet hall at the Skirvin Hotel are, from left to right, George W. Armstrong, Oklahoma City mayor Allen Street, unidentified (background), Todd Storz, and Raymond Ruff. Ruff had been sales manager for KOMA from the mid-1930s to 1952, when he left for other opportunities. He returned as general manager in 1956, then was replaced when Todd Storz bought the station. Ruff eventually purchased KTUL radio from Griffin, changed the call letters to KELI, and brought the Top 40 format to Tulsa.

One of the first promotions was to bury this stuntman at the local Spring Lake amusement park and leave him there until KOMA was number one in Oklahoma City. From left to right are Jack Sampson; the stuntman, who used the name Wa-Chi-Ca-Noka; and KOMA program director Rod Roddy. Sampson later managed the Storz station in St. Louis, KXOK, and was inducted into the Missouri Broadcasters Hall of Fame. Roddy moved to California and found fame as the announcer with the loud sports coats for Bob Barker on *The Price Is Right*.

Several advantages helped WKY. Danny Williams, program director, had been featured on a number of shows on WKY-TV since arriving in Oklahoma City in 1950. He knew a lot of people in the business, such as Wolfman Jack, who visited with Williams on a trip through Oklahoma City. As Williams hired DJs, they were given shows on WKY-TV. The station had the full backing of the *Daily Oklahoman*, so every contest, promotion, and appearance WKY disk jockeys made was fully promoted. They had a fully staffed news department that worked both radio and television.

Danny Williams found Don Wallace at a radio station in Tulsa, already playing rock-and-roll records and doing sock hops. Wallace became the midday DJ on WKY and soon had a hunting and fishing show on WKY-TV. He also conducted sock hops almost every weekend.

Next, Williams found a DJ at a station in Lawton. He heard him on the air and called him on a Saturday afternoon to ask if he could drive up to his home in Oklahoma City on Sunday and visit. Ronnie Kaye could not believe it when Danny Williams offered him a job at WKY. Like many other DJs at WKY Radio, he soon had his own show on WKY-TV. Ronnie Kaye's *The Scene* was a local knockoff of *American Bandstand* but more popular in Oklahoma City television ratings than Dick Clark's show.

DJ Ronnie Kaye congratulates Bishop McGuinness High School cheerleader Betsy Wilson for winning tickets to a Dave Clark Five concert from WKY. At right looking on is WKY DJ Terry McGrew. This was just one of the many contest winners both stations had during the rock-and-roll war. More winners meant more listeners.

The Tom Paxton Show, shown afternoons on WKY-TV, featured rock-and-roll artists and WKY DJs introducing and interviewing them. Above is Gary Lewis and the Playboys, and below are the Dave Clark Five.

From left to right, three of the most popular DJs—Ronnie Kaye, Danny Williams, and Dale Wehba—check the latest Star Survey, the weekly hit list published by WKY. Ronnie Kaye was still on the air at KOMA-FM, while Webha had retired. Webha left WKY to be program director at CKLW, a powerful station in Windsor, Ontario, that covers Detroit. He later came back to Oklahoma City and KOMA.

News was an important element of the popular music format. In 1961, Jack Ogle was hired by WKY Radio as a newscaster. Ogle, who like most of the on-air staff grew up locally, had been doing news at KNOR Radio in Norman, Oklahoma. He moved to WKY-TV after a couple of years on WKY Radio. He was the 6:00 p.m. and 10:00 p.m. anchor through the early 1980s. Ogle began a news dynasty that continues today. His three sons are anchors—Kent anchors the morning newscasts on the NBC affiliate, Kevin anchors the 6:00 p.m. and 10:00 p.m. newscasts there, and Kelly anchors the 6:00 p.m. and 10:00 p.m. newscasts at the CBS affiliate. Ogle's granddaughter Abigail (daughter of Kevin) anchors the 6:00 p.m. and 10:00 p.m. newscasts on the ABC affiliate, and her younger sister Katelyn is a reporter at the CBS affiliate, which is owned by David Griffin, grandson of J.T. Griffin, who owned KOMA in the 1940s and 1950s.

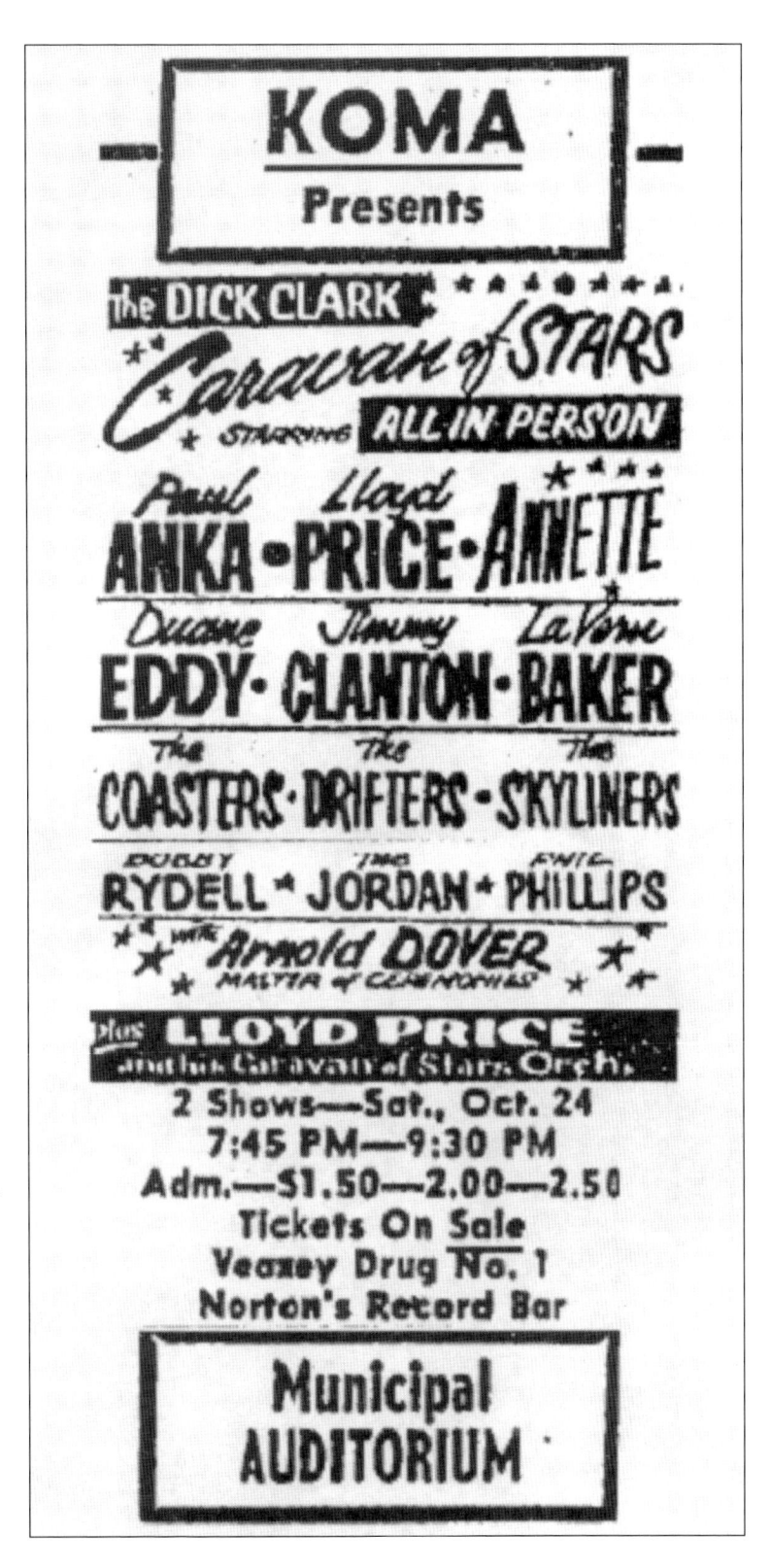

The two stations created alliances with booking companies for the right to "present" recording artists at their concert appearances in Oklahoma City. That gave the station the opportunity to have its DJs actually introduce rock-and-roll stars appearing in Oklahoma City.

KOMA Presents

The Dick Clark Caravan of Stars

Starring — All In Person

Paul ANKA • Lloyd PRICE • ANNETTE
Duane EDDY • Jimmy CLANTON • LaVerne BAKER
The COASTERS • The DRIFTERS • The SKYLINERS
Bobby RYDELL • Jimmy JORDAN • Phil PHILLIPS

with Arnold DOVER, Master of Ceremonies

plus LLOYD PRICE and his Caravan of Stars Orch.

2 Shows—Sat., Oct. 24
7:45 PM—9:30 PM
Adm.—$1.50—2.00—2.50
Tickets On Sale
Veazey Drug No. 1
Norton's Record Bar

Municipal AUDITORIUM

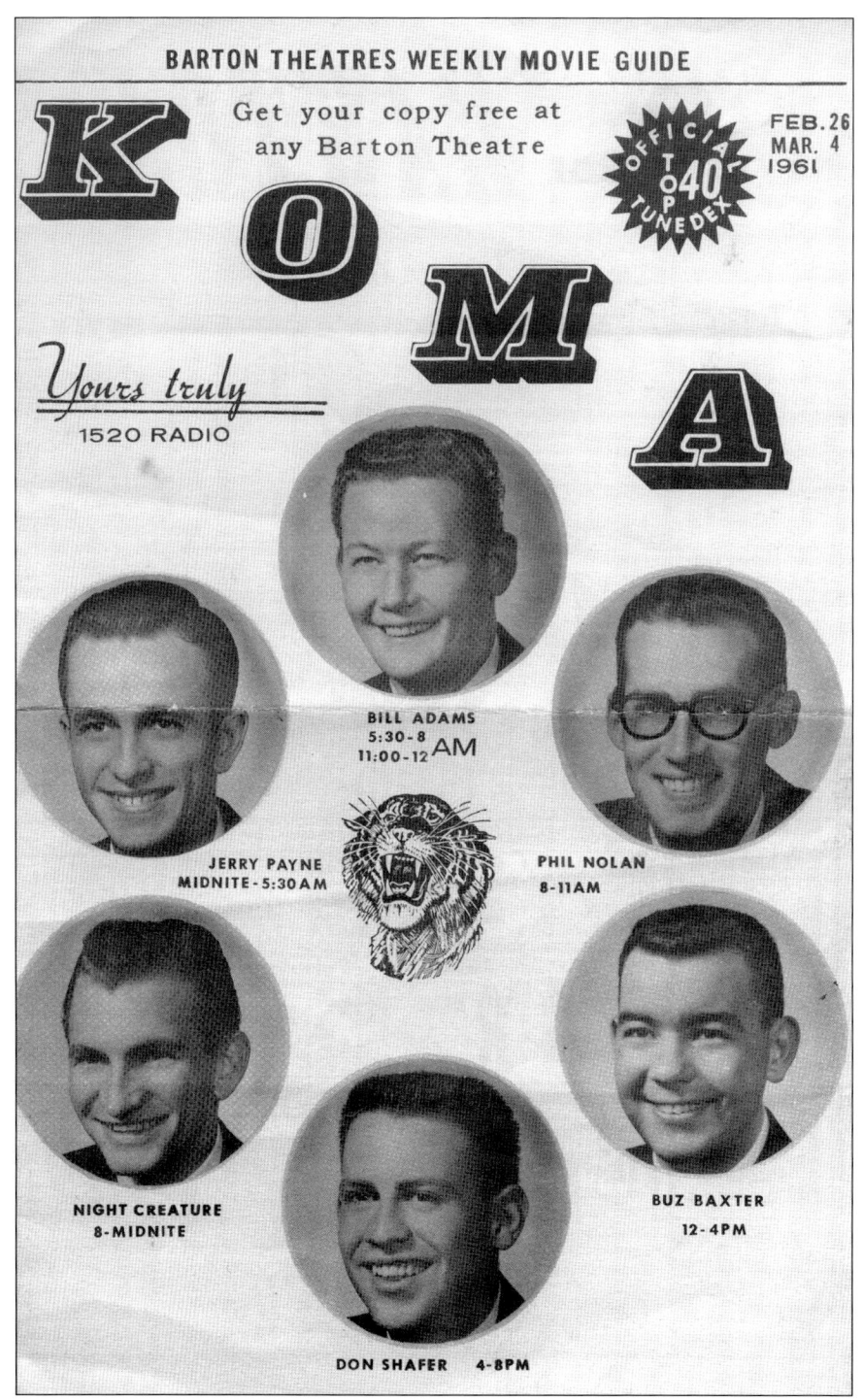

Each week, KOMA and WKY printed a list of the top-selling and most-requested records for that week in Oklahoma City. They were distributed at record stores and dime stores such as TG&Y, which had locations throughout the state. This was a great way to promote the stations and its disk jockeys.

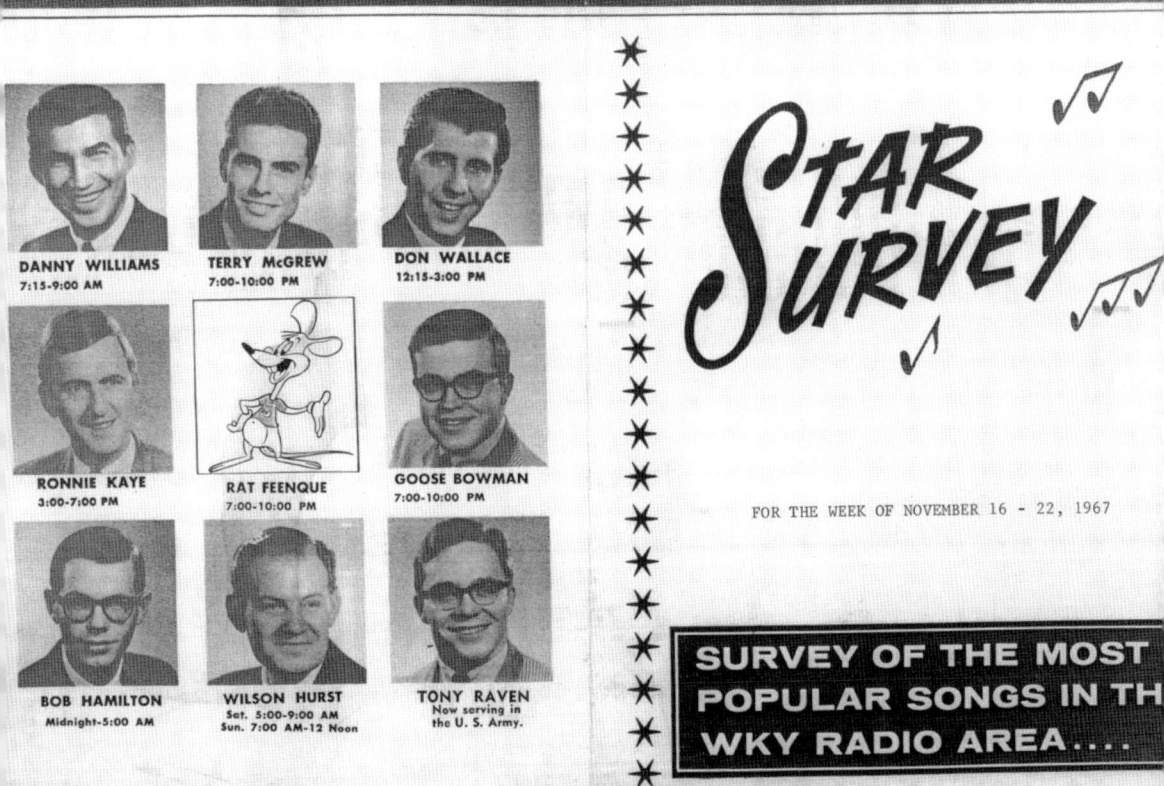

The WKY Star Survey also featured advertising. One of the DJs pictured, Bob Hamilton, began publishing a weekly magazine, the *Bob Hamilton Radio Report*, in which stations shared ideas for promotions, sales ideas for the sales department, and so on. The magazine was very successful and widely read throughout the country. The WKY staff was somewhat different than KOMA in that it was mostly local talent. Danny Williams, the program director, along with Terry McGrew, Don Wallace, Ronnie Kaye, Jim "Goose" Bowman, and Wilson Hurst, all either were from Oklahoma or had lived in the state for some years. In that era, radio stations frequently published weekly record charts with pictures of their DJs. A picture of a DJ serving in Vietnam became common.

A popular DJ on KOMA from 1965 to 1971 was John David. He began there as a weekend DJ while attending Oklahoma State University. After graduation, be became a full-time DJ. Later, he and another OSU graduate owned radio stations in Joplin, Missouri. Since the late 1980s, David has been the vice president for radio at the National Association of Broadcasters in Washington, DC.

Many DJs at both stations used their experience in Oklahoma City as a gateway to larger markets. Chuck Dunaway of Texas found his way to WKY Radio. Danny Williams, Ronnie Kaye, and Dale Webha coached him, and soon, he left for a larger market. He always remembered his mentors in Oklahoma City and comes back to the Sooner State as often as he can. He also had a small role on Danny Williams's television show.

After working the afternoon shift on WKY Radio, it did not take long for Chuck Dunaway to land at the biggest rock-and-roll station in the nation, WABC New York. He served in programming management positions at a number of stations in Dallas, Houston, Cleveland, and other markets before moving into ownership. He and his wife teamed up to buy and turn around failing radio stations.

Among the DJs who came through KOMA were local talents such as Chuck Dan, who grew up and started in radio in Duncan, Oklahoma, and Machine Gun Kelly, who was from McAlester, Oklahoma. Chuck Dan, who was later a voice-over talent in Los Angeles, came back to KOMA under his real name, Charles D. Hanks. Michael D. Hanks, who is currently a prominent voice-over talent in Los Angeles, followed his brother at KOMA in the early 1970s while a student at the University of Oklahoma.

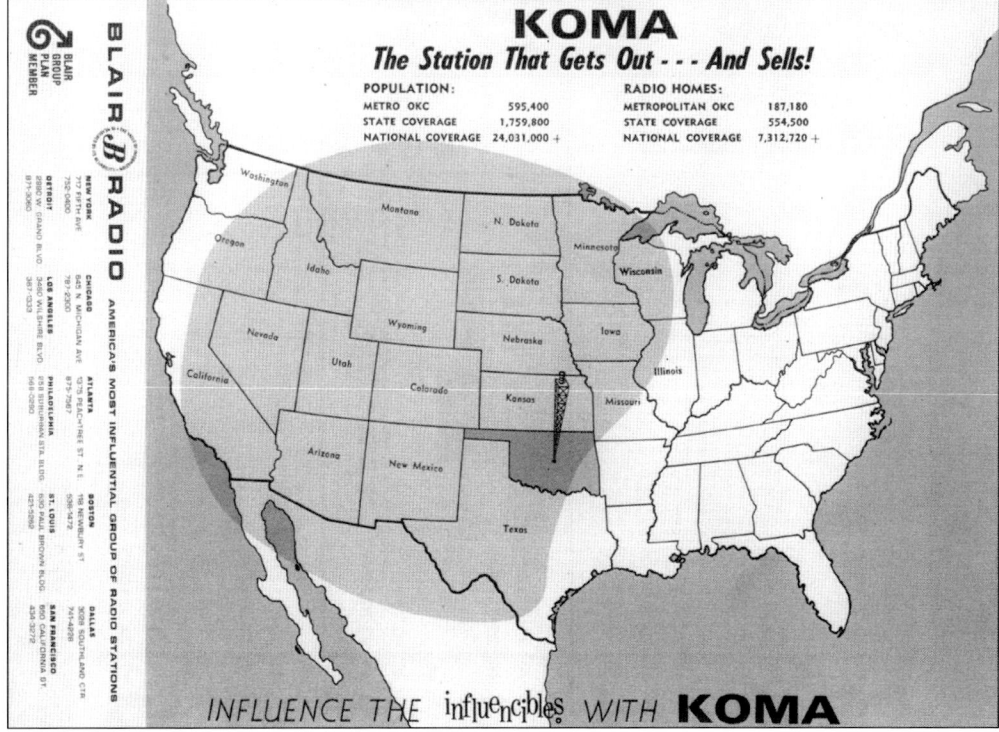

This brochure image shows the enormous nighttime signal KOMA blasted over the western two thirds of the United States. In an annual survey, KOMA consistently had the second highest listenership in the country through the 1960s. KOMA often was rated the number one station at night in local ratings in cities such as Lincoln, Denver, Phoenix, Amarillo, Albuquerque, and Santa Fe. While KOMA had a gigantic national audience, the station seldom beat WKY in Oklahoma City.

Nearly all the early Top 40 DJs at KOMA used the station as a gateway to larger stations in larger markets. Todd Storz, who always promoted from within, asked Phil Nolan to move to his station WDGY in Minneapolis. After a long career in broadcasting, Nolan was inducted into the Minnesota Broadcasters Hall of Fame. The other DJs pictured on this 1961 KOMA roster had equally great careers in broadcasting. "Night Creature" was one name given to the automation machine that ran on the overnight shift. Internally it was referred to as "Silent Sam." Todd Storz built that machine and many other pieces of equipment used at his stations.

Four

THE DAY THE MUSIC DIED

Given that both WKY and KOMA began featuring local country music bands in programs in the late 1930s and 1940s, it would seem logical that Oklahoma City listeners would be treated to full-time country music by the 1950s and 1960s as music format stations became the norm. But it was not until the early 1970s that an FM station adopted country-and-western music as its format.

Beginning in the late 1950s, Jack Beasley formatted his daytime-only AM station, KLPR, as a country-and-western station. As a "Daytimer," KLPR signed on at 6:00 a.m. but had to sign off at local sunset, a time that changed each month and was prescribed in its FCC license. That placed KLPR at a strong disadvantage in competing with other stations in Oklahoma City.

Around 1970, KEBC, an FM station with studios on the south side of Oklahoma City, went country. Gene Wingate, general manager, believed that a full-time FM station playing country could beat a daytime-only AM station and that country music fans would make the move to FM.

This was the beginning of the FM radio revolution. Until the early 1970s, the few FM stations that were on the air mainly played the "beautiful music" format and used slogans such as "Where FM means Fine Music." Around this time, baby boomers were discovering that the fidelity of the FM signal was better for all kinds of music, not just beautiful music; auto manufacturers began installing AM-FM radios in their cars; and station owners began trying different types of music to attract listeners.

One of the earliest FM stations was WKY-FM, which went on the air July 1, 1947. The station broadcast classical music, and programming was kept separate from WKY-AM. By 1952, management decided to shut the station down because there were no FM receivers. The transmitter and equipment were donated to the Oklahoma City Public School system for its use. That station, on 98.9, came back to life in the 1960s and 1970s under several different owners and call letters; today, it is known as KYIS, owned by Cumulus. KTOK-FM went on the air in the late 1940s but later went off the air. Station 101.5 went through several ownership changes and formats. That station came back to life in the late 1950s as KIOO. In 1970, though, Jack Beasley bought it, changed the call letters to KJAK, and began playing country music with his daytime AM station KLPR. In 1976, it got new owners, and they changed the format to album rock and the new call letters KATT.

Another well-known FM station is KJYO at 102.7 on the dial. This station began in the 1960s as KJEM-FM with its AM brother KJEM 800. It played adult standards until 1972, when the station became KAFG and ran the Drake oldies format. Then in 1977, it became KZUE, "The Zoo," playing contemporary hot hits. In 1979, KOFM adopted the same format and took the Zoo's listeners. In 1981, it picked up the easy listening format as K-JYO (or K-JOY, the Joy of Oklahoma). After the company that owned it became Clear Channel Communications, it changed to KJ-103, playing hot hits. With these and other FM stations doing well, by 1975, when managers added up the total listenership on AM versus FM, the percentage of listeners on FM exceeded 50 percent. That was bad news for the AM stations and good news for FM. FM had finally come alive.

Some companies were left behind. In the early 1960s, Todd Storz had envisioned the day when FM stations would rule. He told his managers that someday, Oklahoma City would have 20 or more radio stations. And when asked where those stations would come from, his answer was "FM. That's the future of our business." He died in 1964, and his father, Robert Storz, took over the company. Robert was a businessman but lacked the imagination and creativity his son had. When FM licenses were available, he ignored them. He never filed for a new FM station. By the mid-1970s, Storz Broadcasting was on its last legs, and ultimately, the company vanished. Gaylord Broadcasting gave up its FM license and did not file for another one. The station went through a number of formats—country, talk radio, easy listening, news talk—but none if it worked. Thus, WKY struggled and was left in the dust.

In more recent times, the FM licenses for Oklahoma City have all been taken. A new approach for broadcasters became "move ins." About a dozen FM stations in Oklahoma City are actually licensed to other communities but have their studios here. Many are owned by local companies successfully broadcasting not just to Oklahoma City but also to their community of license. This includes stations licensed to Enid, Anadarko, and El Reno.

The advent of AM Stereo in the early 1990s was supposed to save AM, but because of various technical issues, it never took off. Sports talk and political news talk formats have worked to some degree in rehabilitating the ratings of a few AM stations.

Ralph Tyler began working in radio while in high school in Okmulgee, Oklahoma, then moved to Oklahoma City to attend college and found work at the dirt track on the Oklahoma State Fairgrounds announcing the Saturday night races. Race fans said they really enjoyed his announcing style and the enthusiasm in his voice. That launched Tyler into being hired as a booth announcer at KOCO-TV, the ABC affiliate that had just moved to Oklahoma City from Enid.

This tight-knit group eventually became well-known Oklahoma City broadcasters: From left to right are Bill Howard, Mike Water, Ralph Tyler, HoHo the Clown, Bill Thrash, and Jerry Oor. Bill Howard was a longtime producer at KOCO-TV, Mike Waters did the same, HoHo was the best-known children's entertainer on Oklahoma City television, and Bill Thrash was the senior program producer at WKY-TV.

Though Ralph Tyler had played country music at a radio station in Okmulgee, working at KOCO-TV brought him into the Oklahoma City country music scene through the station's *Action Wagon*, featuring the Swinging Conner Family. They were one of the more popular country acts in Oklahoma City in the 1960s and early 1970s. Here, Tyler is the announcer, along with Ida B., who was hostess on several shows at KOCO-TV, while HoHo is on the right. Tyler left the station in the late 1960s and opened an advertising agency serving the small mom-and-pop stores on the south side of Oklahoma City. He served a niche market the larger agencies would not touch.

Ralph Tyler was placing large amounts of advertising on KEBC, whose studio and office were in a barn-style building at 830 Southwest Thirty-First Street. Through the early 1970s, he placed thousands of dollars of advertising with the station. The station was supposed to reimburse him with a discount for being an advertising agency but could not pay him back. Eventually, Tyler and Gene Wingate agreed for Tyler to become an owner of KEBC. Ultimately, he became the sole owner.

Part of Ralph Tyler's advertising business had included signs on bus stop benches, so he began using them to promote his radio station. The station did not have a slogan until one Sunday morning an announcer heard one of the preachers who bought time on the station close his program by saying, "This is Brother So and So saying Keep Every Body Christian." The announcer told Tyler they should starting saying, "K-E-B-C—Keep Every Body Country." And the station's slogan was born.

Ralph Tyler found a number of ways to make his station family-friendly and thus build ratings, including with this miniature fire truck. Oklahoma City held several parades every year, and the KEBC disc jockeys would ride in the parade on the back of the fire truck. The fire truck was featured at several amusement parks in Oklahoma City during KEBC events. It was quite popular at Spring Lake and Wedgewood amusement parks.

Kenneth Johnson wrote and broadcast a Sunday morning program on WKY Radio titled *Creed, Color, and Co-Operation*. Johnson was a student at Langston University, Oklahoma's university for black students, when he went to the WKY program director, Hoyt Andres, with the idea for the show. Johnson told Andres he had contacted many civic leaders and had letters from them supporting the idea of a radio program for blacks. Andres was quoted in the *Daily Oklahoman* as saying the program would spotlight instances of progress in relations between the races. In 1948, *Billboard* magazine awarded the program second place in the nation as a public service program.

Ben Tipton became the leading voice of Oklahoma City's black community as a broadcaster in the 1960s. Born in Oklahoma City, Tipton graduated from Douglas High School. He was tall, at six feet, five inches, and played basketball in Arkansas. He later joined the Navy and became interested in communications. Returning to Oklahoma City, he began working at KBYE and quickly became one of its most popular DJs. In 1970, he left Oklahoma City to work at WLS, the ABC-owned radio and television station in Chicago. Within a year, he returned home to continue his career at KBYE.

Tipton developed KBYE-FM, and the station rocketed to number one in the local ratings, but because of a power struggle between the white station owners and black employees at KBYE, Tipton publicly resigned from KBYE. His next stop was KOCO-TV, where he hosted a weekly review of black news in Oklahoma City. In 1969, *Movie Mirror* magazine named Tipton Top DJ in the Nation. In 1977, Tipton was elected to the Oklahoma City Council and served until 1981. He died of cancer in 1988.

In 1970, the Oklahoma City Community Action Program (CAP) honored Russell Perry, owner of the *Black Dispatch* newspaper; Ben Tipton; and Kay Dyer with special awards presented by Jerry Mash, president of the CAP. Dyer was a community activist working for civil rights in Oklahoma City in the 1960s.

In the late 1950s, Douglas High School had an outstanding quarterback named Russell Perry. Oklahoma Public Schools were still segregated, but Perry led his team to victory against the all-white Capitol Hill High School. That marked one of the first football games between a black school and a white one. Perry later attended the University of Maryland Eastern Shore on a football scholarship. After graduation, he returned to Oklahoma City and began his business career, which included founding the *Black Chronicle* in 1979. In 1993, Perry purchased what had been KLPR and changed the call letters to KRMP, the Touch 1140. He later purchased a station in Anadarko, west of Oklahoma City, and a station in Tulsa.

Five

TODAY IN OKLAHOMA CITY RADIO

Two of the three largest radio ownership companies own stations in Oklahoma City, and two locally owned groups also have multiple stations here. iHeart Media, formerly Clear Channel Communications, headquartered in San Antonio, owns 855 radio stations in America. It is the largest radio station group owner in the United States, both by number of stations and by revenue.

iHeart Media in Oklahoma City owns KGHM 1340 AM, sports; KYJO 102.7 FM, Top 40; KBRU 94.7 FM, rock; KTOK 1000 AM, news/talk; KTST 101.9 FM, country; KXXY-FM 96.1, classic country; and El Patron 98.5, Spanish language.

Cumulus Media is the third-largest owner and operator of radio stations in America. The company, headquartered in Atlanta, Georgia, owns 446 stations in 90 markets. In Oklahoma City, Cumulus owns KATT-FM 100.5, album-oriented rock; KKWD 104.9, rhythmic Top 40; KWPN 640, sports talk; KQOB 96.9, adult hits; KYIS 98.9, hot adult contemporary; WKY 930, Spanish language; and WWLS-FM 98.1, sports talk.

Tyler Media is owned by Ralph Tyler and his sons Ty and Tony Tyler. Ralph began the company as an advertising agency serving south Oklahoma City and then bought a country-and-western FM station in 1971. KEBC became the number one–rated radio station in Oklahoma City within just a few years. His sons attended Dallas University after graduating from high school in Oklahoma City. There, they discovered the power of Spanish-format radio and television and brought that to Oklahoma City. With the success of the Latino stations, Ralph purchased a group of stations from Tony Renda, a Pittsburgh-based broadcaster. Tyler Media is the Oklahoma City partner in Sooner Sports Properties and is the Oklahoma City broadcaster for University of Oklahoma athletics. They carry all Sooner football games, men's basketball games, women's basketball games, and various other sports. The Tyler stations include KEBC 1560, sports; KOKC (former KOMA) 1520, news talk; KTUZ-FM 106.7, regional Spanish language; KRXO-FM 107.7, sports; KMGL 104.1, adult contemporary; KOMA 92.5, classic hits; and KJKE 93.3, country music. In addition, the Tylers also own two Spanish television stations. One is affiliated with Telemundo and the other with Univision.

Perry Broadcasting was founded by Russell M. Perry and is owned by him as well. Perry grew up in Oklahoma City. In 1979, he started the Perry Publishing Company with the first edition of Oklahoma City's *Black Chronicle*. The newspaper, a weekly periodical serving the Oklahoma City metro area's African American population, has grown into one of the largest paid weekly papers in the state. Currently, it serves the entire state of Oklahoma including Tulsa, Lawton/Fort Sill, and Oklahoma City. In 1993, with the purchase of KVSP 1140 AM in Oklahoma City, Perry formed the Perry Publishing & Broadcasting Company Inc. KVSP AM became the first urban-formatted radio station for Oklahoma City in more than 15 years.

Perry Publishing & Broadcasting Company is the largest independent minority-owned-and-operated radio broadcasting company in the United States. In Oklahoma, Perry owns KVSP 103.5 FM, urban contemporary; KACO 98.5 FM, hit/hot country; KJMZ FM 97.9 Jamz, urban contemporary; KDDQ FM 105.3, mainstream rock; KPNS AM 1350, conservative talk; KKEN FM 97.1, kickin' country; KXCA AM 1050, national sports talk; KKRX AM 1380, adult R&B/soul; and KRMP AM 1140, adult R&B/soul. Perry also owns stations in South Carolina and Georgia.

As can be seen from this list, 1520 KOMA is now KOKC 1520, news talk, and is still locally owned. WKY is La Indomable, Spanish sports talk, and is owned by a company in Atlanta.

DJs from 101.9 The Twister (contemporary country), visit local high schools on Friday nights to host tailgates at their football games. This visit was to the suburb of Wellston before a game.

Several times, *America's Got Talent* scouts have held auditions in Oklahoma City. KJ103's disk jockeys (from left to right) TJ, JRod, and Janet are pictured doing a remote broadcast from one of those audition sessions, where they interviewed contestants.

From left to right, the Twister's Steve Rosen, Kathi Yeager, and Buff host the Oklahoma City Country Cares for St. Jude Kids Radiothon. They raise thousands of dollars each year for this charity.

Joining with the Oklahoma Highway Safety Office are, from left to right, KJ103's JRod, Janet, and TJ, urging their listeners to pledge not to drive impaired.

KJ103 DJ Janet "From Another Planet" is doing a remote from the library in one of Oklahoma City's high schools promoting reading.

Cumulus Radio owns several stations in Oklahoma City, including WWLS The Sports Animal. The crew hosts an annual charity golf tournament in the name of Bob Barry Jr. (or BBJ as he was known on the air), who was tragically killed in a traffic accident. He was extremely popular on the sports talk station and was the sports director at KFOR-TV, having replaced his father when he retired. The crew raises thousands of dollars each summer, which is then donated to various charities.

On location doing a remote on WWLS 98.1 FM The Sports Animal are Emanuel Rivera (left) and Gideon Hamilton. They are entertaining a young family of listeners at this remote.

The three "Afternoon Animals" are on WWLS at the Texas State Fair in Dallas before the annual OU-Texas football game. The game is played at the Cotton Bowl Stadium on the fairgrounds during the middle weekend of the fair. Broadcasting are, from left to right, Jim Traber, Dean Blevins, Al Eschbach, and three unidentified. The three have been in sports talk radio in Oklahoma City longer than anyone else in the market.

Ralph Tyler, founder of Tyler Media, has been joined by his sons Tony (left) and Ty Tyler (right). After graduating from an Oklahoma City high school, the sons headed south and both graduated from the University of Dallas. While in Dallas, Tony and Ty discovered Spanish radio. They found Oklahoma City had a large Latino population, so they have gotten into Spanish/Mexican-format radio in Oklahoma City.

Pictured here is the KTUZ annual remote and stage presentation at the University of Oklahoma for Day of the Dead. Mainly taking place in central and southern Mexico, this weeklong celebration remembers family and friends who have passed and helps them through their journey. With the opening of Spanish-language stations, this celebration has become very popular on the OU campus.

KMGL Magic 104, Oklahoma City's adult contemporary music station, holds a Spring Fling around Memorial Day to say goodbye to winter. Thousands of listeners show up for this annual event.

Another Magic 104 event each spring is the annual Easter egg hunt. A city park is the location, and the kids and their parents flock to it. This is one of the many family-friendly events Magic 104 holds throughout the year.

KTUZ, one of the Tyler Media Spanish stations, holds an annual Z-Fest each summer. This photograph shows how popular Spanish programming has become with an audience that had been ignored by Oklahoma City broadcasters for many years.

One of the Tyler Media country stations is Jake FM. Each summer, it holds a Jake Jam in a park near downtown Oklahoma City. Many people show up, and fun seems to be had by all.

Magic 104 holds a toy drive every December, with thousands of listeners donating new toys that are given to needy families. This crew is getting ready to drive to one of the drop-off locations to load this truck with newly donated toys.

The Franchise 107.7 is one of the Tyler Media stations that features sports talk. Tyler Media is also a partner in Sooner Sports Properties from Learfield Sports, which owns the broadcast rights to all University of Oklahoma athletics. This is one of the two tailgate locations for the franchise before home football games. The OU football broadcasts are among the three football radio programs with the largest audiences in college football.

Discover Thousands of Local History Books
Featuring Millions of Vintage Images

Arcadia Publishing, the leading local history publisher in the United States, is committed to making history accessible and meaningful through publishing books that celebrate and preserve the heritage of America's people and places.

Find more books like this at
www.arcadiapublishing.com

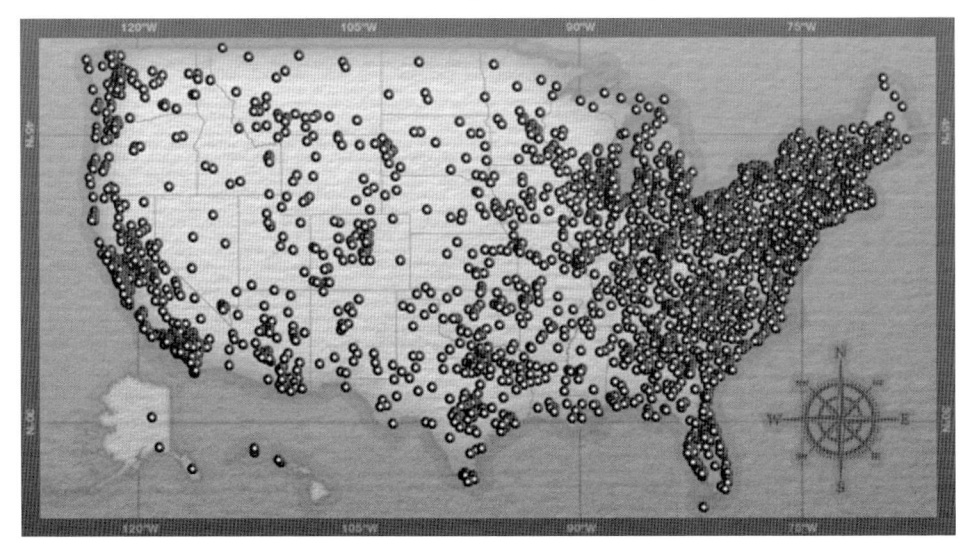

Search for your hometown history, your old stomping grounds, and even your favorite sports team.

Consistent with our mission to preserve history on a local level, this book was printed in South Carolina on American-made paper and manufactured entirely in the United States. Products carrying the accredited Forest Stewardship Council (FSC) label are printed on 100 percent FSC-certified paper.

MADE IN THE USA